SWAT

by
Jim Ollhoff

VISIT US AT:
WWW.ABDOPUBLISHING.COM

Published by ABDO Publishing Company, PO Box 398166, Minneapolis, MN 55439.
Copyright ©2013 by Abdo Consulting Group, Inc. International copyrights reserved
in all countries. No part of this book may be reproduced in any form without written
permission from the publisher. ABDO & Daughters™ is a trademark and logo of
ABDO Publishing Company.

Printed in the United States of America, North Mankato, Minnesota.
052012
092012

 PRINTED ON RECYCLED PAPER

Editor: John Hamilton
Graphic Design: Sue Hamilton
Cover Design: Neil Klinepier
Cover Photo: iStockphoto
Interior Photos and Illustrations: AP-pgs 1, 4-5, 6, 7, 9, 13, 15, 16-17, 18-19, 20,
22, 25, 26-27 & 28-29; Combined Tactical Systems-pg 12; Glow Images-pgs 8 & 14;
iStockphoto-pgs 3, 20-21 & 23; Thinkstock-pgs 12, 13, 16, 24, 30 & 32.

ABDO Booklinks

To learn more about Emergency Workers, visit ABDO Publishing Company online.
Web sites about Emergency Workers are featured on our Book Links pages. These links
are routinely monitored and updated to provide the most current information available.
Web site: www.abdopublishing.com

Library of Congress Cataloging-in-Publication Data

Ollhoff, Jim, 1959-
  SWAT / Jim Ollhoff.
    p. cm. -- (Emergency workers)
  Includes index.
  ISBN 978-1-61783-517-9
  1. Police--Special weapons and tactics units--Juvenile literature. 2. Hazardous
occupations--Juvenile literature. I. Title.
  HV8080.S64O45 2013
  363.2'3--dc23
                        2012009527

TABLE OF CONTENTS

SWAT TEAM

A crazed man enters a bank and pulls a gun. He waves the gun around, demanding money and shouting commands. He barricades himself inside the bank, threatening to shoot hostages if anybody comes too close.

Police get an order to arrest a violent criminal. They know that when they find him, he will have guns and bodyguards, and that he will resist arrest.

Four terrorists hide out in a room in a large apartment building. They are building bombs that will cause innocent people to suffer injuries and death. If police rush in too quickly, the terrorists could set off the explosives and destroy a large part of the building and hurt anyone inside.

These extreme situations require special tactics and weapons. They require men and women who have received specialized training and can move with perfect teamwork. These extreme situations need a SWAT team—an elite team of men and women who are trained in Special Weapons and Tactics.

A police department's SWAT team responds to a bank robbery in Chicago, Illinois, in 2007.

SWAT HISTORY

During the 1960s, violence was becoming more of a concern than ever before. There were several sniper attacks across the country, in which crazed people with high-powered rifles started shooting people. Domestic terrorists began building bombs and threatening to do damage.

With new kinds of criminals and new kinds of weapons, police departments knew they needed a new approach. They needed a highly trained, disciplined team to deal with these very dangerous situations. The Los Angeles Police Department was the first to train officers to respond to high-risk emergencies.

The idea caught on across the country. Soon, SWAT (Special Weapons and Tactics) teams were formed in nearly every state. Over time, SWAT team responsibilities began to include rescuing hostages and arresting dangerous criminals who might fight back. Today, SWAT teams are present in most large cities in the United States. Most developed countries have SWAT teams.

Above: Smoke rises from a sniper's gun at a University of Texas tower in 1966. Below: A security officer stands at the spot where a sniper killed 16 people at the University of Texas-Austin. The sniper was killed by police. Attacks like this highlighted the need for trained SWAT (Special Weapons and Tactics) teams.

WHAT DOES A SWAT TEAM DO?

The main job of a SWAT team is to enter dangerous situations, and then resolve them—peacefully, if possible. SWAT teams work hard to protect all people, especially innocent citizens.

SWAT teams are called on to handle many different situations. If people are taken hostage, a SWAT team is called. The team works to keep other people safe so that more people aren't taken hostage. They make sure the building is surrounded so that the hostage-takers can't escape. They talk with the hostage-takers to try to get the hostages released safely. In some cases, the SWAT team may have to burst in and forcibly rescue the hostages. This is more dangerous, but sometimes it may be the only choice.

SWAT teams provide an extra line of defense when important people come to a city. For example, the president of the United States is protected by the Secret Service when visiting a city, but a SWAT team may provide extra security. Any time there is some kind of special event in a city, there may be a need for extra protection.

A Dallas, Texas, SWAT team member carries a hostage from an apartment building after the girl was released by an armed man in 2003.

9

When protests get out of control, they can become riots. Rioters can destroy property and injure innocent people. In these cases, SWAT teams can be called to help maintain order and protect innocent people.

Sometimes police must get a warrant. A warrant is a kind of permission, usually issued by a judge, that allows police to arrest people or search their property. Most arrests happen without a fight. However, some people will resist arrest. They may barricade themselves in their

house or hideout, and have a lot of weapons to try to stop police from arresting them. In these situations, a SWAT team may be called.

SWAT teams train a lot. Since SWAT teams must act together and move in precise fashion, they need to train together. In some areas, SWAT team members are also police officers. When members are called, they need to leave their role as traditional police officers, and get ready to work as a SWAT team.

A SWAT team in riot gear is called in to handle angry protestors in Albuquerque, New Mexico, in 2003.

WEAPONS AND EQUIPMENT

SWAT teams use many different kinds of weapons. Their main job is to keep innocent people safe, and resolve dangerous situations peacefully. In order to do this, many of their weapons don't use lethal force.

FLASHBANG

Also called a stun grenade, a flashbang is like a very large firecracker. Police can throw it into a room, and when the grenade bursts it lets out a bright flash and a very loud bang. This surprises people and disorients them. It is hard to see or hear for several seconds after a flashbang goes off. Flashbangs are often tossed into a hostile room right before a SWAT team enters.

A flashbang is detonated during a training exercise.

Tear gas is used to disperse an unruly crowd in Oakland, California, in 2011.

TEAR GAS

This is a canister of gas that might be shot into a room where criminals have barricaded themselves. The gas spews out, causing the eyes to tear up. It can cause a lot of eye and nose pain, and even temporary blindness. It is very difficult to stay in a room where tear gas is spewing into the air. Sometimes tear gas is used to disperse large crowds of rioting people.

STING GRENADES

These are sometimes called hornet's nest grenades, because when they go off it feels like walking into a giant hornet's nest. When a sting grenade goes off, it shoots  out a lot of tiny rubber balls. The balls bounce off of hard objects, so someone standing in a room can get hit from every direction.

NIGHT VISION GOGGLES

SWAT teams often wear these goggles at night or in a building that is very dark. The goggles gather and intensify light, enabling the SWAT team members to see in dark places where criminals cannot see well.

A policeman wearing night vision goggles.

K-9 UNITS

SWAT team members sometimes get help from specially trained dogs. Dogs have a better sense of smell than humans, and can often find people who are lost or hiding. Dogs can run faster than people. They can chase down criminals who are running away. One of the most common breeds of police dog is the German shepherd. A German shepherd is big and strong, and can tackle a criminal and hold him in place until police officers arrive.

A German shepherd is trained to take down and hold a suspect.

TRAINING

It is a source of pride and prestige to be on a SWAT team. SWAT team members are selected from local police units. It's important that SWAT team members know the police policies and procedures for their area.

Physical fitness is an important part of SWAT training. SWAT members keep in top shape by including exercises such as weightlifting and long-distance running. Agility exercises are also important since SWAT officers never know what kind of situations they will face. They have to be physically ready at all times.

SWAT members have to be mentally ready, too. They have to think fast, but not recklessly. If they are reckless, they might get themselves or someone on their team hurt or killed. SWAT team members learn how to act in dangerous situations, and to follow orders and procedures. They have to trust other people on their team, and know that they will always protect each other.

In a SWAT training exercise, a Harrisonburg, Virginia, police officer searches an abandoned building for an armed suspect. SWAT team members are trained to follow orders and procedures, but also how to think fast and perform carefully even in extremely dangerous situations.

SWAT members learn to become expert shots. They spend hours learning how to shoot at a target. They have to learn how to shoot when they or the target are moving, or both. They need to know how to use all their weapons and tools, and which ones are most appropriate in any given situation. Sometimes that means hand-to-hand defensive tactics, too. They have to be ready for anything.

SWAT team members also have to learn psychology so they can better understand what a criminal may do next. They have to communicate well with their team, and with people involved in hostile situations.

Some SWAT members can pursue other kinds of training as well. They might be trained in how to defuse explosives. They might learn

how to be long-distance snipers. They might be trained in how to negotiate to free hostages.

Many SWAT training sessions are called simulations. A simulation is a pretend situation that is made to seem real. For example, they may use an old, abandoned house, pretending that a criminal is hiding inside. They have to practice entering the house. Mannequins might spring out at the SWAT team members. They have to decide if the fake attacker is a criminal or an innocent bystander. Simulations are never perfect, but they can help officers learn to think fast. Good officers learn from mistakes made in the simulation, so they can be better in real-life situations.

SWAT teams are constantly training. There is always something new to practice. There is always some skill at which the team can improve.

SWAT team members cross a runway at Castle Airport in Atwater, California. The training exercise includes a terrorist takeover of a 737 airplane. The simulation tests the team's skill in a highjacking situation. It also includes detonating an explosive device by bomb squad members.

STRATEGY AND TACTICS

In any dangerous situation, the goal is to have a peaceful ending. The best scenario is where the subject gives up or can be pinned down and handcuffed. SWAT weapons, gear, and training are designed to confuse criminals or make them scared enough to give up. That's the best way to end a standoff. In fact, more than 90 percent of SWAT calls end without anyone firing a single shot.

But what if there is a criminal hiding in a building, and he is holding a hostage? The criminal has a gun and threatens to start shooting. The first thing a SWAT team does is try to contact the criminal and negotiate with him. But what if they can't talk to him? What if the criminal refuses to pick up the phone?

A SWAT team plans a mission in a command center vehicle.

The SWAT team leader may then decide that they should enter the building. They move toward the door, in single file. When they are in single file, all except the front person present less of a target. The officer in front is not only the one most at risk, but is also the one who has to make all the quick decisions. The team might burst open the door with a heavy battering ram, and then enter the room with guns drawn. They all duck down and face different directions. They are trying to cover different parts of the room. The direction they look is called their area of responsibility. This way, they can see all areas of the room quickly, without getting in each other's way.

If the team knows where the criminal is, they might throw a flashbang grenade into the room. When it goes off, they may rush in and tackle the criminal.

Sometimes, the situation does not end peacefully. Sometimes someone has a gun and is firing aimlessly. These criminals are called "active shooters." They cannot be reasoned with or talked out of their actions. Negotiation is impossible because the shooters are actively firing at people. These situations are extremely rare, but when they happen, SWAT team members know they may have to kill the shooter.

The body of a shooter is lowered from a rooftop.

When the situation is finished, the danger is gone and the injured are taken to the hospital. But there is still more for the SWAT team to do. They have to sit down and talk through what happened. They need to learn from their mistakes and understand if anything could have been done differently for a better outcome next time.

Whatever happens, the SWAT team members are there to maintain order and keep people safe. That's their job, and they take it very seriously.

INTERVIEW WITH A SWAT OFFICER

Eric LeBlanc has served in a large suburban police department in Minnesota for 17 years. He holds the rank of sergeant. He has been a SWAT team member for 13 years, and is the SWAT team leader. He also trained as a police sniper and a crime scene technician.

Q: How did you get interested in becoming a SWAT officer?

LeBlanc: SWAT interested me because of the important role that it plays for all police departments. Being a SWAT officer is like being a regular police officer but with very specialized equipment and training that is used during dangerous situations. The specialized training and equipment is what interested me most. Utilizing these tools and skills in a high risk and high stress environment sounded exciting and challenging. Saving people's lives is the first priority of a SWAT officer.

Officers prepare to enter a house where a killer is hiding.

A SWAT team surrounds a bank where a man is held hostage.

Q: What is a day like for a SWAT officer?

LeBlanc: The average day of a SWAT officer consists of a lot of training. A significant amount of time is spent at the firing range becoming proficient in the use of all the assigned weapons. In addition, there is a lot of time spent practicing with the tools assigned to the team. Just as an athlete practices, so does a SWAT officer. Mock entries into homes, schools, and businesses in order to arrest criminals and save lives are examples of our training.

Q: What has been a memorable experience?

LeBlanc: One of the most memorable experiences was when I was training as a sniper in the Florida Everglades. On the fifth day of training, we were sent out to find a place to hide from our instructor. I found what I thought was a perfect hiding spot, then all of a sudden I discovered that I was lying on top of a fire ant nest! As the ants began to sting me, I jumped up and ran from my hiding spot yelling! The instructor thought I was joking around and yelled at me. Then he saw me take my pants off and fire ants were all over my legs! Then he stopped yelling at me.

Q: What's the best part about being a SWAT officer?

LeBlanc: The best part is that each day of work offers you an entirely new experience. You go on different calls and deal with different kinds of people almost every day. The job is never boring. Of course, helping people when they need assistance is a great feeling too. There is no better feeling than when a citizen tells you, "Thanks for all that you do to keep us safe."

Q: What can kids do who want to become SWAT officers?

LeBlanc: The things that are important today will be really important when you want to become a police officer and join a SWAT team. Be an honest person. Treat your parents, teachers, friends, and all people with respect. Be a good student and listener. Be a leader. Challenge yourself to be the voice of reason when your peers think about doing illegal or dangerous things. Read a lot and become the best communicator that you can. Volunteer to help people in any way you can. Good luck!

SWAT members train to handle the detonation of explosives in Roswell, New Mexico.

GLOSSARY

BARRICADE

A barrier created by using whatever materials are on hand. Barricades prevent living things or vehicles from coming or going from certain areas.

DEFUSE

To take the fuse out of a bomb or other explosive device. Also, to stop a violent situation from becoming worse.

FLASHBANG

A grenade that gives off a very bright flash and a loud bang. This stuns people for a few seconds.

LETHAL FORCE

Force strong enough to cause the death of a living thing.

NEGOTIATE

When two opposing sides discuss a situation and agree to a compromise. Each side has gotten some things they want and each has allowed the other side to get some of what they want.

PSYCHOLOGY

The study of the human mind and how it works. In police work, psychology is used to figure out what a criminal might do in certain situations, and then use that knowledge to stop the criminal.

SCENARIO

A sequence of events that could happen, and the order in which they may take place.

SIMULATION

A pretend situation that helps officers learn what to do in a real-life situation.

SNIPER

A person who has deadly aim with a gun from a long distance.

STING GRENADE

A grenade that has rubber balls in it, which bounce at very fast speeds and hit targets from all angles.

TACTICS

A plan of action designed to achieve a specific outcome. SWAT team members plan the tactics they'll use in dangerous situations, such as freeing hostages or disarming criminals.

TEAR GAS

A gas, spewed out of a canister, that makes people tear up and gives them pain in their nose and eyes.

TERRORIST

A person who uses violence, or the threat of violence, to get what he or she wants.

INDEX

SWAT members training on a shooting range.